OH!
How We Sometimes Miss Ourselves

TSIETSI KUAHO NKONDO

authorHOUSE®

AuthorHouse™
1663 Liberty Drive
Bloomington, IN 47403
www.authorhouse.com
Phone: 1 (800) 839-8640

Published by AuthorHouse 02/09/2016

ISBN: 978-1-5049-7293-2 (sc)
ISBN: 978-1-5049-7295-6 (e)

CONTENTS

THE JOURNEY BEGINS

Sitting in this family car with my children following the hearse carrying the casket in which my wife, their mother eternally lies, a replay of a similar occasion is replaying itself in my head. It is not long ago that I attended a funeral of someone who had a tremendous impact on my life. I am immersed in a strong feeling of de'javu.

This time it is my wife who is being buried. Then it was someone whose name I did not know, but my thoughts raced to the occasion of his burial. Today I feel like the centre of this occasion, unlike then when I was just a face in the crowd in an occasion that had all the making of a pauper's funeral, a funeral that had no chief mourner. This one is classy and full of pomp; the cartage is made up of expensive cars of note. I was calmer than is usually the case on such occasions of bereavement. I had to be strong and calm for the sake of the kids or maybe even for myself, ironically this did not take much effort. Something had prepared me for this and I was prepared.

I am not sure if one can prepare oneself for the death of a beloved; but looking at and observing the outward demeanour of the bereaved during the ceremonies of burials, I sometimes – I daresay always – think it is possible to emotionally prepare your innermost for such occasions. It is the inevitability that makes it imperative to consciously or sub-consciously be prepared. The serenity prayer should be the idea to espouse and apply it in its totality and relevance to life's happenings particularly in a moment like this one. I do not know its source, but it begs for courage, serenity and wisdom.

If one has prayed it and own it, I think it is a tool that we all should use. To what effect, would depend on ones level of inner honesty. On the previous occasion the funeral was more of a lesson than bereavement. Then I was on the outside looking in through the window, but now I am on the inside and am the centre of the happenings.

There are things that are vivid in my mind which actually contribute to my present state. Then, when I looked at the cars ahead of the one I was driving in, particularly the simple hearse, I felt bare and unsophisticated. Today this moment of bereavement is shrouded in what I regard as blatant pomp and a high level of sophistication. Funerals always have a way of revealing our inner vulnerability to which we are normally sorely oblivious of.

Then, I was feeling gratefully sad. I was grateful that I was there but saddened by my powerlessness for the moment. My emptiness was very much fulfilling. I wished my dry tears would be wet and visible. My cheeks were understandably expecting a tepid drop to fall on them, my handkerchief was ready should I feel my eyelids unable to contain my tears. I am supposed to be mourning; actually I am expecting to feel a lump in my throat, it feels right and appropriate to mourn. Today I do feel that lump. It is acceptable and expected to unashamedly shed a tear at such moments and occasions.

The time I knew him and the moments I spent with him, among many other things, made me realise how much death reveals in all of us. My mind raced and my memory rewound to the times I spent with him, more so now that I am the centre of this occasion of bereavement.

I was in the second year of study at college when I started taking note of him and paying attention to his presence. He was a groundskeeper with an astonishing presence. His physical outwards appearance was very ordinary, nothing eye-catching to warrant your eyes to stay on him for any length of time

There was something, though, about his body movement and general demeanour that demanded attention. The way he turned his head, the way he picked up or put down the tools he worked with, the way he removed his hat when he was about to wipe his brow. His demeanour was literally tangible and palpable to a discerning eye. Everything about his body movements was compelling. There was something regally unusual about him, a groundskeeper nevertheless.

His movements were not exaggerated, they were effortlessly measured and polished, gentle but deliberate, and there was nothing uncouth about any movement he made. This is about all that one could pick up from a distance.

Those who bothered to be close to him and to pick a conversation with him experienced his deep, strong, authoritative but gentle voice. His voice was the kind that put you at ease and comforted you no matter how greatly taxing you imagined your situation to be.

His eyes were talking, gentle but intense. They had a soothing stare that gave solace to a troubled soul. They seemed to know the silent language used to ease a heavily laden and muddled mind.

There was something about him that I just could not put my finger on. Suffice to call it "that thing "or merely "something"

He was not the one who would talk about himself or his family. I even wondered if he had any. Maybe that is what made his funeral such a simple affair. There were only four cars excluding the simple hearse and the battered bus. There was some singing coming from the bus, some sympathetic sounding funeral hymn as though rendered by a choir that never rehearsed together if at all, a hymn nonetheless.

I tried to match the man to the singing coming from the bus. On the outside and from the distance one could be pardoned to strike a match. But to me, knowing him as I did, the man behind the face, the inner man behind the appearance, this was a blatant mismatch.

In my mind he deserved a choir of angelic voices to honour his final farewell or welcome home, whichever way you looked at it. I wonder where and who makes or takes such decisions.

My first one-on-one encounter with him was quite early in the year, before the college's first short vacation. He always saw a group of us young students passing noisily and we did not take any notice of him. His outward appearance, to me then, did not demand that of us. It was a chilly windy day and he was raking fallen leaves, papers and a variety of loose lying debris that were littering the college grounds.

We were on our way to the campus main chapel for a memorial service of one of the student leaders who had died in a car accident.

The service turned out to be very emotional, maybe this was made so by the popularity and the stature of the deceased. The student, mainly the females, could not contain their sorrow and most were weeping openly. The mood was sombre and the chapel engulfed in mourning.

As my eyes darted around, I caught a glimpse of his family members. They were shrouded by gloom and hurt. The mother and one of the sisters were a sight that one wished never to see again. The pain of loss was written all over them. I subconsciously put my family in their place and this had a devastating effect on me. My whole life played itself bare in my mind; the little boy inside of me got engulfed in the misery and mystery of death and bereavement.

I wanted to talk to somebody about this matter; I wanted to engage with somebody, just to hear what some people made of this thing called death. This "phenomenon" as somebody would say.

Just by the way, I thought I understood why you would find people whispering, chitchatting and fidgeting during such occasions and making a nuisance of themselves. I think it is the only way open to them to steer away from thinking about the realities of death on their lives. This is their way to escape and free their minds from what death would mean when it came knocking at their door. The little child in them is scared to face it as it really is.

I had a lot of questions about life and death but did not have the means, the art or the ability to articulate them. I did not know if I was wondering about what life was or what death was. I wanted to ask, how do we die? What is this thing called death? Why do we die? Is there a way to deal with death? How should the living relate to death? I wondered if all these questions really had answers or if they mattered at all.

The sermon delivered by a retired minister could have contributed to this state I found myself in. The theme for this sermon was "all is vanity." I wondered if all was really vanity, the relationships we get into one-on-one or as groups, how we choose to relate to each other, all these things called virtues, were they also vanity?

I did not think of death as an academic subject, it was to me a real life feeling…. vanity maybe. This did not need a PhD in Social Sciences nor Philosophy, neither did it need anything in the line of academic divinity. These fields would surely yield facts and theories about what was troubling me, but would not do justice to the feeling itself. I was troubled by a feeling. I again wondered if this was not the vanity that the minister was preaching about.

At the end of the service there was a lot of greetings and chitchatting about this, that and nothing from the crowd as is always the case on such occasions. The mood of the occasion was soon brushed aside to be replaced by the normal jovial mood of campus life. People were instantaneously in the "life-must-go-on" mode. The girls who not so long ago were such a heart rendering and mournful sight to watch, had undergone an unbelievable emotional metamorphosis as they giggled and gave one another high fives.

As we dispersed I wanted to avoid the noisy company I came with. This company that I normally enjoyed had all of a sudden turned vexatious. I wanted to be alone with my thoughts. The comfort I sensed in the simple old man manning the grounds filed my head. I sneaked into the restrooms to buy time and to make sure that I was left behind. I wished I could be in his comforting and reassuring presence and this filled me with a pleasant feeling of blissful déjà vu.

When I looked at the face staring back at me in the mirror, I could not understand the expression on my own face. I looked scared and confused. This Halloween looking face that resembled me could only be mine because I was alone in there.

I could sense the little defenceless boy in me, and oh! How I pitied him.

As I went out, the chapel was almost deserted. The road outside leading back to the residence had few people as the majority of people went in the direction of the campus' recreation facilities. These were in the opposite direction to the residences.

I wanted to get to my dormitory to get myself together, to be like everybody. I needed a moment of solitude to collect the scattered me.

As I looked ahead of me, I saw him cutting a lone figure that resembled a predator lurking to ambush its unsuspecting prey. Deep down in me I knew the troubled inner me was that prey. Inwardly I wished I could be swallowed into his inside which to me seemed so calm and serene. I yearned for calm and I thought his inside was full of this very calmness. As I approached him from a distance, his body language was welcoming and I felt like screaming in anticipation of relief. The confusion in my head was reaching boiling point, what is this thing called death; the question was reverberating in my head.

WHAT IS THIS THING CALLED DEATH

We went through the irritating and time consuming exchange of pleasantries. I thought it very impolite to shower him with my concerns without first going through these formalities. I do not remember how and what words I used to present my case to him. What followed convinced me that he got me loud and clear.

He sat me down and started talking as if talking to himself but being very mindful of my presence.

Death is the flip side of life, he would say. Death is not the end of life but the beginning of the other form of life. This made me lift my eyebrows in awe. If it was the end then the departed would be erased from our memories, don't you also think so? He would ask, but because it is not so, it is not the end, the memory of the departed live forever in us. Put another way, the dead live, yes live forever in our minds. This does not depend on whether they were close friends or distant enemies. They all live forever in our minds. Death is thus the transformation of man's state of being, from the visible ending and perishable form to the unending everlasting indelible form.

The impact and value of this form is going to be largely influenced and determined by the quality, worth, meaning and the character of the life that was before death. In life we are in death and in death we are also in life, so the saying goes.

The way we regard and think about life come into operation and influence our perception of death. Whether we accept death and celebrate life or we for any reason whatsoever, internally deny the reality of death thus painfully prolonging and delaying the inevitable acceptance thereof is dependent upon the realities and appropriateness of our philosophies in life about death or upon the occurrence of death about the life that preceded it.

Our existence is a two sided coin, one being life and the other death. We call it life because that is the side we are consciously experiencing.

There is nothing right or wrong about death, so also about life. It is only about all we make of it.

Death comes when it comes, expected or unexpected. How we perceive it, gives it a particular and specific meaning to us. This perception is in turn formulated and influenced by factors, both physical and mental, that we have been exposed to since birth during the different stages of our mental growth. This mental journey through the different stages of life has a direct influence on the perceptions we end up owning, either about life or death or both.

Whether we take the route of being locked up in the pain of self pity and hurt that is commonly and habitually linked to death, or whether we consciously come to terms with it and move on, is totally dependent on our life-view, self-image, perceptions and the meaning we have attributed to this phenomenon.

If he suspected that I was having a problem following what he was saying, which was rarely the case, he would change gears trying to come to my level and would continue saying:

Life is like a long distance journey on a bus, train or any form of public transportation. The duration of the journey is determined by the destination printed on our individual tickets. Some go far some go near. Some people find us in the bus, this bus that is life, and leave us on the bus as it reaches their official destination as displayed on their tickets. We also find some in the bus and leave them therein as the bus reaches our destination. It is not always the case of first-in-first-out, or last-in-last-out, or last-in-first-out, or first-in-last-out. The bus will always stop for some to come in and for some to go out. In the same way, people disembark the bus of life when it reaches their destination which is marked 'Death'.

As he was talking I was trying to make a link between what he was saying and logic as I understood it. I was trying to make sense of this and not the vanity that the sermon was all about?

Any two or more of the travellers may be engaged in a common topic en route or may start playing a game of chess or droughts. You might enjoy one or more games to their end. You might also not finish a single game because arriving at your destination signals the end of any game that you could be engaged in. It does not matter how much you enjoyed the company of your fellow travellers. Your physical company comes to an end when anyone of you reaches their destination printed on the ticket.

The fortunate or unfortunate part, depending on how one looks at it, is that in the case of life, the destination is printed with invisible ink that only the conductor of the bus of life can read. When your name is called there is no way to alter, modify or prolong the stay in the bus.

Harmony on this issue is contained in realization of the biblical passage that says *"Show me, Lord, my life's end, and the number of my days, let me know how fleeting my life is."* that I may gracefully leave the bus when my destination is reached, despite the joyous company I enjoyed in the bus.

This is true to the games we play in life. For as long as the journey continues and we are interested, we can play. For as long as the curtains are up we continue acting. When the curtain falls, or should I say when the curtain is dropped, all actors go backstage. Whilst on stage there are two visible sets of people and the third is invisible and inevitable. The creators and directors of the play are not visible but the cast is always under their control.

All the stage utterances and manoeuvres are predictably known in advance by the creator and director, but not to the audience. When the curtain falls we are away from the eyes and presence of the audience but now present with the director to evaluate and possibly get feedback of the stage performance. At this stage we stop playing for the audience. We get backstage where everything started. The stage part has ended but the person who carried the stage character has not ended. He takes the backstage form.

When death comes it signals the change. The change which is away from the eye of the audience, ceasing to be the character you were playing, abandoning the stage image and taking the backstage status. The traveller's stage has passed with all the travellers' activities (games, championships, etc.). Once was a traveller in the transport, now a guest at the destination. Once was an actor on stage, now myself backstage.

This, simply put, is the nature of death.

You could be back stage and in your head you still hear the applause of the audience. You could even still be feeling the satisfaction that your acting gave you or your audience. This satisfaction you can still cling to long after the curtain has fallen.

This is where your joy hangs – whether on stage or backstage. When the acting has ended, you can choose to enjoy what lingers on your mind, the feeling ingrained in your memory. This you can own and hang on to whether you were part of the audience or part of the cast.

Similarly, those that formed part of the audience are going to remain with lingering memories of your performance. This performance is what you were to them. They are going to remain with the impact that your life had on theirs. These could stem from the blissful feelings in hindsight from sweet memories of the past or bitterness resulting from bad blood that existed during your moments of contact.

I got it very loud and clear. I was not sure if he was talking about life or death. What he said addressed that confusion I was feeling, it really made sense and to me it said what we made of death is dependent on our life experiences with the departed and our own perception about the relationships we found ourselves in and the impact it had on us.

Could we prepare ourselves for death so that we are not mesmerised and unduly hurt and broken by it when it strikes or when it comes? …..

My next big question was about how relationships affect our reaction or response to death.

On this day of his funeral as I look at the nonchalant demeanours of the small crowd of people in the cortege, I felt greatly offended by it. I felt the loss, but it looked like I was the only one feeling so. I tried all I could to hide my gnawing feeling of loss about his death. My eyes darted around looking for a face I could find solace in, to help me say to myself, I am not alone.

Was he really this insignificant to all these people here? Did I allow myself to be too close to him emotionally? These were the questions that darted in my head like moths around a glowing lamp, irritatingly present but with no meaningful or effective results.

When the simple coffin was lowered into the grave, the brave outside of me was in strife with the grief stricken inside of me that had this connection with him. I knew that during the burial rites his name would be mentioned and it dawned to me that I never knew his name. Amidst this confusion I made sure not to miss it. He called everybody "Moshate", The Royal one. There was nothing royal about all of us but when he looked at us he saw this Royalty, and he expressed it boldly. To me he had this unrecognised Royalty that he bestowed upon each one us. You could feel it in his voice when he spoke.

I hurriedly searched my pockets for a pen and took out my pocket diary. I did not want to miss his name. I would be hearing it for the first, and probably the last time. Maybe someone would mention it again later, and I wanted to remember it should this happen. I wanted to put the name to the character that influenced my thinking and emotions so much.

Whether I would appear like a newshound scavenging at even the menial of occasions for scraps of news to feed to gossip columns or like a police or intelligence spy, it really did not matter at this moment. I wished I had a voice recorder to capture what was said about him, where he came from and why he found himself here.

Although very little was said, in gluttony I absorbed every little morsel of information that was said about this man who to me was larger than life. I had to rely on my memory for the encounters I had with him. His name, even if it meant scribbling it on my dry forearm or the ground, this I would do. My pocketed diary came out handy and I waited. I found myself silently eulogizing about a man who opened my eyes about the realities of life and living and of relationships and relating.

This is the man who instilled in me the knowledge that it takes two to tango when it comes to relationships. Any union or partnership is brought to an end firstly by the demise or death of both or either of its members or secondly by the members never ever having come together at all, *ab initio* as some people would understand it.

Of these two scenarios, the first was easy to understand, it is the second that needed some unpacking.

In his effort to bring me to understanding; he used an example of a marriage. This is where he asked us if we ever wondered why people divorced, actually why divorce is so rife in the lives of couples who externally portray a picture of a match made in heaven?

As I looked around and seeing couples that had come to attend his funeral, I could not help but see them being separated by either death or divorce. At this moment I remembered what he said about both.

Why people die is a matter that no man had control on, it is a question that is best left to the supernatural or divinity. What we could look at, with a great measure of success, is why people permanently stop belonging whilst both are still alive.

One of the worrying thoughts that we had to wrestle with was prompted by the separation of a married couple who, to most of us, was an epitome of a match made in heaven. This couple was an envy of all and sundry within the student population and, I dare say to most of their colleagues. When news of their impending divorce started making rounds first within the campus, they were met with great disbelief. It was especially unthinkable and a very hard thing for our youthful minds to fathom.

Yes they were about to divorce and there was very little that anyone could do about it. A big question was latched into our minds and needed something or some one to unlatch it. The question was, why do people divorce?

WHY DO PEOPLE DIVORCE

He is the one who told us how binding relationships evolve, they are not instant. People can live ages together without bonding, he said. Mere physical togetherness does not ordinarily give rise to or result in bonding. Unless personal boundaries are broken and cease to exist, no bonding will take place. One should bear in mind that such boundaries are in most cases jealously guarded against outside invasions of any kind and for any reason.

Our personal boundaries would naturally insulate us as a means of protecting us from anything from our outside and this includes from one another. We all remain distant faces in the crowd *ad infinitum* until some volunteered revelation has taken place. This revelation starts from the point of removing insulating personal barriers and boundaries and laying the inside of you bare and at the mercy of some particular instance or individual.

This means revealing and exposing your true inner and outer ever-changing self to the other person, this to either your own peril or to your glorious bliss. This ever-changing self comes about when the outer you is continually adjusting to be in sync with deep imbedded inner you. If this does not happen you remain a faceless presence in the midst of people or to the one in your life.

Is this then what he was to all these people gathered around his grave? I wondered, a faceless presence in the crowd, without any emotional identity or consequence as a result of the personal boundaries that insulated him from the rest of us.

On this occasion when we wondered about why people divorced, he assured us that it is because they have married without having met. The persons on the inside of persons have not met, resulting in the persons on the outside not bonding. He went on to explain and this is how I understood him.

Each one of us has got a protective hedge around us that single us out from the rest. A group of people with a common purpose are further encircled together by a common broader hedge. This could be any of the multitudes of groups that are separated from the rest by virtue of the common factor that separates one group from the other. Their communication and social intercourse is strictly dictated to by their membership guidelines. This group of people are engulfed by the common identity that makes them belong. This common identity could be the home, the church, the profession, the political formation, a fan-club, or any other congregation of individuals with a specific defined common purpose.

How close they can relate to one another is determined by the common cause. Each remains safe within his personal space. All people in the same military rank relate in an identical manner to anyone holding a rank higher than theirs.

All children in the family say "Papa" or "Daddy" in the same way to their male parent. They deserve protection and provision in the same like manner. As they grow and their uniqueness become evident, the father's approach towards them takes an individualised approach. Looked at from a distance, one may mistakenly think that, some become more equal than others or some are favoured above others.

Schematically this is how I understood him

1

TOTAL STRANGERS.

You start as total strangers possibly knowing nothing about one another save that which brought you to this proximity.

This is the first point of contact which does not necessarily need to be physical. It could be **a** voice over the phone, **a** blogger on the internet, **a** person serving you or being served by you at any point of service, **a** face in an assembly of any sort either as a regular or a visitor, this list is endless.

Here you see and recognise **a** person's name or face or both, but are not in a relationship of any noteworthy or particular kind or consequence but merely as determined by the nature, rules, practices and expectations governing this setting.

This arms length relationship may stay like this forever without developing into a noteworthy phase, or it may out of necessity, decency or interest escalate to the following level.

2

CLOSE BUT NOT INTIMATE

At this point you have some kind of knowledge of the person, albeit limited to and by the setting in (1) above. You may get into some kind of one-on-one discussion, but mostly at arm's length with nothing intimate. Depending on the aura flowing from such an individual, you may be somewhat attracted for intimacy or outright repelled. This is the point where you consciously or unconsciously start gauging the other person for compatibility. This is the most crucial moment, as the saying goes, this is where the rubber hits the road.

You miss it here, then you are in for a rough ride.

It is here where the stage is set for the kind of relationship that this is going be. Absolute and undiluted honesty about self and the other person on the envisaged progression of the relationship is an essential prerequisite.

Life view, ambitions, spirituality are but a few of the virtues that must be tacitly or deliberately vigorously scrutinized at this stage.

The next stage is entered into based on the assumption that this ground work has been honestly done.

This is the stage where, rightly or wrongly, assumptions are made for a possible progression toward a possible lasting relationship. You know the other person but you do not miss their company. This is where you weigh the possibilities.

If one is, for whatever reason, under some pressure for intimacy, this is where hurried decisions toward intimacy are taken. If not, the stage is now set for a smooth progression to the next level.

3

INTIMATE WITH LIMITED SHARING

This is where the two of you start missing the other person's company. You yearn for the other person's presence for what it does to you. In their absence you are overcome with the after taste of their fulfilling presence next to you. Your mind is inundated with the thoughts of making appointments for being together.

The outside world start noticing your being together and the spark in your eyes starts being obvious. Those around you start asking questions and you become aware that your intimacy is becoming visibly real.

You start sharing things and your time to a limited extend. If not influenced by external factors, you enjoy this sharing and giving and do not feel compelled or guilty if you don't.

Most friendships are at this level where the two of you are separated from the group. You start introducing each other to kith and kin.

You start being free and comfortable in each other's company

4

INTIMATE WITH VISIBLE SHARING

Your intimacy is intense and you both declare your undying urge to stay inseparable. You see it in each other's eyes and hear it in your voices when you talk.

You each nevertheless want to make sure whether losing yourselves to each other is the thing that the other person will be comfortable with.

You are prepared to take a dive with your body and soul.

5

INTIMATE SHARING

You have made peace with your souls that you belong together. You have come to the level where you freely share everything. Sharing goes beyond personal external possessions and goes to sharing the selves. Temptation for sexual intimacy/intercourse is very high and whether or not this does take place will be at the mercy of both the moral convictions and virtues of the two of you.

6

INSEPARABLE DECLARED SHARING

Marriage at this level is unavoidable because it has proven futile to try to continue living in separate camps.

7

TOTAL UNITY

You are now two hearts that beat as one. Her concerns are your responsibility and your concerns are her responsibility. There is nothing that stands between you, not your jobs, not your families not even your children.

8

SHARING LIFE

When you encounter each other away from the physical enclosure that binds you, your terms of reference will be subjected to the known bond that makes you belong. Your discourse and reasons for living will be limited to the reason that brought you together.

In each other's absence, the one fills the shoes of the other. "You hear the one you've heard the other, you see the one you've seen the other". They live for what they are to one another.

The time it takes for this bonding to be a reality is by no means dependant on the time the two were exposed to one another, for some it takes a surprisingly very short time, whilst for others it take ages.

But truth be told, when all is said and done, better than this you cannot have it.

The only thing that can defeat and throw the above progression into disarray and throw it into the quagmire of misery, is deception, deception of self or others. This deception, for any reason, by both or by either one of the two people is a sure recipe for heart ache and nuptial disaster.

I remember the saying that goes something like:

You can fool some people some of the times and

You can fool some people all the time

And you can fool all the people some of the times

But you cannot fool all people all the time

This is nothing in comparison to fooling yourself and living a life of deceit.

Why do relationships crumble?

This is the question that went through my mind as I was standing reading notices at the one High court just the other day.

This question refers to relationships and partnerships of any kind including but not limited to business and marriages.

I came with the answer that, it is because the parties have not met at their core.

The outer persons or structures seem or are deemed to be together whilst the inner persons (juristic or otherwise) have just not met.

When the initial outer excitement ceases to hold or when the dust settles, as is inevitably the case, the inner person kicks in. It is only at this late stage that the reality of a mismatch comes to the fore.

You try to search for the person you thought you are partnered to and you find a total stranger.

The crucial journey of life has hit a snag and there are no prospects of forward or upward mobility. You do not know who you have partnered yourself to. You wish to start afresh.

You do not know who you are married to, you do not know this person who is your spouse, your business partner, your team mate, the list goes on and on.

There are many factors that cause people not to reveal their true selves to the outside world.

Trust and Transparency are at the forefront of these factors.

You cannot reveal yourself wholly to a person or persons you do not trust and you cannot trust a person who is not transparent to you.

Honesty begets Trust, Trust encourages Transparency and Transparency attracts Trust and so the circle goes.

The key, therefore, is honesty:

Honesty about your shortcomings: If you get into a partnership, at the heart thereof is, or should be, that the partnership should make up for your shortcomings. The partnership is hamstrung and cannot be of any benefit to either or both parties if shortcomings are hidden or not disclosed, either by deliberate and conscious commission or by sheer unintended omission.

Honesty about your fears: If get into any partnership, marriage included, a display of macho bravado is the undoing of such a partnership. We all without exception have a fear of something. It could be a fear of heights, water, embarrassment, failure, closed up areas, loving or anyone of the many things out there. If we do not make known our fears, however insignificant this disclosure seems to us, this poses a nemesis to whoever we have partnered with. As a result of such nondisclosure such partnerships are doomed to failure from the onset or in future.

Honesty about your aspirations..........
Honesty about your faith........
Honesty about your temperament........
Honesty about your life-view..........
Honesty about your past.........
Honesty about your plans
Honesty about yourself........

Need I say more? Honesty in all areas of your life

Take the life's mirror and take a serious look at your INNER self and give an honest feedback to whomever you want to share part of or the rest of your life with.

How do you shape? He would ask us, sounding somewhat morckingly sarcastic although his caring voice unmistakeably reassuring us in our confussion.

SUNDAYS

Today was a very busy day for a Sunday.

It was not busy because any special thing happened.

I just looked at it with a very special and different eye.

People hurried to church the normal way that they usually do.

Today I focused on the expressions on their faces.

What I observed really left me with many unanswered questions.

I saw very few happy faces.

Faces of people in a hurry.

It did not appear to me as though they were fulfilled by what they were doing.

They were like people on an errand forced on them……

People in a trance………

Busy on a collective "make believe"……

The cars were sparkling ....

Their occupants nicely and immaculately dressed.....

Most faces wearing these hollow nonchalant expressions...

I wondered if they are in control of what is happening to them....

Or they are just pawns executing predetermined moves....

For acceptance and the sense of belonging.....

Conforming to the status quo.......

People in some auto-pilot mode .....

It seemed to me the Husbands were doing it for the wives...

The wives for the Husbands.......

The parents for the Children....

The children for the parents........

All because they were raised to know that it is the right thing to do

WE ARE WINESKINS

In the olden days wine was not bottled as is the case today but was kept and preserved in leather made pouches called wineskins. You would be correct to regard them as leather bottles.

When wine is put into wineskins, it maintains its quality and improves in taste.

However, this will remain so for the lifespan of the wine in this particular wineskin. With the fermenting of the wine, the wineskin stretches to the limit, assumes a rigid shape and loses flexibility. With the passing of time these very wineskins become brittle. When after some time one puts new wine into these wineskins using them the second time, there is a great risk of the wineskin bursting

The loss that is incurred is great in that you lose both the wine and the wineskins.

There is, therefore no wisdom in trying to re-use old wineskins for new wine.

In like manner, when one is faced with new ideas, you cannot use them on the old you or you cannot use the old you on them. There has to be a renewal taking place.

This renewal takes place in the different aspects of your life.

Your life view should change to be on par with the new ideas so as to yield improvement.

If you get into a new relationship, of whatever nature, you've got to change your outlook in order to conform to the demands of the new relationship. You cannot give the new relationship the old you.

If you get into a new venture, in like manner, you should change and align yourself and your thinking to the new set of rules needed to execute the venture successfully.

If you get into a new relationship, you should shed the old non committed you and embrace the new you that is on par as required and demanded by this new relationship.

If you get into a position of leadership, you should change and renew your thinking from that of a follower to that of a leader.

When you become a parent, you cannot continue with life like a dependent child and raise your children like a child.

When you get into your own business, you throw away the employee mentality. You stop reporting to your boss and start reporting to your work.

Nobody talks to you about your work, you get into and are guided by an intense goal oriented self-talk.

Have you lately checked what is still old in you and needs realigning, changing or completely discarding?

Each one of us owe it to ourselves to stop boasting unduly reminiscing about "the old good days" which have long stopped being of any good to the present.

SELF DECEPTION

What we all are is a result of our self talk. We can only achieve what we tell ourselves. Our dreams are fashioned along the lines of our knowledge, fears and aspirations.

The knowledge that we display has been acquired from sources that filled the environment which raised us. Our thinking and our perceptions are all fashioned along the lines of the thinking of the families that raised us, the communities in which we were raised and the exposures we were part of.

It is just unfortunate that many of us believe and accept what the world has told us about ourselves. Whilst we are battling to decipher who we really are, the world around us has readymade answers of who we are.

The schools we attended had traditions which we associated with and which made us to want to belong. As a result we inadvertently assumed the identities which had nothing to do with who we really were. Our young, innocent and trusting minds were polluted with false identities of ourselves, crafted by well intending adults who themselves were wrestling with fathoming their own true identities.

This unfortunate state of affairs entrenches the strife between the inner person in you and the outer person in you. The harmonious balance, that is the mainstay of success, fulfilment and happiness, is sacrificed. We end up being very good at camouflaging the true us, lest we be tacitly ostracised and sidelined.

For fear of being hurt or ridiculed we strive to master the art of camouflaging our true inner self. Before we can do this successfully, we must first internalise the lie and believe it. We must first deceive ourselves wholly before we can convince the world. This is self deceit.

Is it then not true that there are many of us out there in the world who exist in camouflaged modes? ? In so doing we are always sending all the wrong signals about ourselves to the outside world.

We have acquired the use of fashionable and accepted vocabulary that has nothing to do with who we really are but has everything to do with who we wish to be seen as.

The world then responds to us based on the signals, verbal and otherwise, that we have sent out and not on who we really are.

Don't most politicians and desperate salespeople operate in this manner? Their utterances are heavily punctuated with sloganeering that appeals to their audiences albeit at the expense of their own convictions. They replace and exchange the truth for popularity and acceptance

This without doubt leads us to our camouflaging ourselves to our own downfall.

BURIED ALIVE: THE SELF ENTOMBED

Thinking of him, out of nowhere an Idea flashed through my mind.

This is an idea of boulders that we have allowed to entomb us, lock, stock and barrel, with all our dreams, ambitions and aspirations.

We all have experienced incidents and have been part of practices that have had us entombed in misery that has rendered us unproductive. It has turned us into a state of unhappiness which has given us a self-picture of hopelessness.

Some of us ended up being drug addicts, alcoholics, ending up with broken dreams, homes and marriages.

We started loathing who we are. There is darkness all around us and these boulders are exerting an increasing pressure of mental uselessness. We have surrendered our fate to unknown forces of doom and decay.

Is this where we belong? Oh no. Not if we can help it.

Remember the "THRILLER" Video? Yes the one by MJ.

There is a sound that can restore you. This sound that can release the giant in you. This sound can release the monstrous energy that has been laying fallow in the inside of you.

This sound can enjoin you with likeminded people who are tired of being entombed. There is a sound out there that is causing people to lift themselves out of their Tombs of misery. One by one they come out free. They enjoy the freedom that has always been there for them to enjoy. They have pushed aside the boulders that have denied them the freedom and pleasures that life has always had in store for them.

Listen to the sound and come out your tomb. This sound has the proven power to EMPOWER you. The power to bring sunshine to your situation.

Yes the boulders are heavy (they were meant to be), but not impossible to remove.

Listen to no one who says you cannot come out. Those are the naysayers who buried you alive.

Their victory is in your staying entombed and rotting.

Your victory is in your coming out. Believe me when I say, everyone can come out, yea even you can come out

ALONE OR TOGETHER

It is not uncommon to hear people saying they
did it on their own. Is this really true?

Coming to think of it, I ask myself if
this is really a fact. Is this true?

Doing it alone, strictly speaking, is not possible… so it cannot
be true that one can succeed singlehandedly.

My thinking is influenced by a number of wisdom statements
from different cultural backgrounds.

I will share but a few of them with you here:

"A Single bracelet does not jingle "This
is a Congolese proverb.

How true is it? Is life not all about the
sweet jingles? Indeed it is.

The sweet romantic jingle between a
couple fills the heart with warmth.

The jingle in the family between father, mother and their children. The pleasure of belonging and knowing that you are never alone is the fuel that drives one to greater heights.

These heights are the jingle, the sweet sound of achievement.

"A single stick may smoke, but will not burn"

There is nothing wrong in physically going it alone, but you do need ideas from others to fire up your actions.

These ideas you can get through reading and having great minds beefing you up on your endeavours.

These are the sticks that can turn you
into a celebratory bonfire

You need mentors, those that have done it before, to fill you with confidence and courage. You can also create mentors from those that failed, from whose experiences your can know what route not to take in your life. This will ensure the warmth of achievement that we all are in search of.

Is it not also true that "In the desert of life the wise person travels by caravan, while the fool prefers to travel alone"

This is so true to anyone who wishes to make it in any business. This includes those that are on Internet Business.

The Internet Rivers and waters are turbulent to those that try to go it alone, trying to reinvent the proverbial wheel all alone. There are caravans that you can easily hook up with.

There are willing and experienced caravans that
are currently making great strides, you only
have to search, discern and get hooked up.

Just look up and sideways, help is at
hand for those who seek it.

There is really nothing to fear because: "Cross the
river in a crowd and the crocodiles won't eat you".

Considering these wise sayings:

"When spiders unite they can tie up a lion"

"Two ants do not fail to pull one grasshopper"

"If you want to go quickly, go alone. If
you want to go far, go together"

"Brothers love each other when they are equally rich."

Alone is not an option, together is the way to go.

IS BEING DOWN BAD?

Life is a combination of valleys and mountaintops.
At any given time we inadvertently find
ourselves at any point between the two.

One man's valley might be another man's mountaintop
depending on one's personal dream and life view.

What is certain is that:

DOWN is not a curse...

Down is not final......

Down is not negative....

Down is not out ....

How you regard your state of being out is all within
you, it actually depends on your attitude.

What IS is simply that, it IS.

How you relate to it is squarely dependent
on you and what you make of it.

Being down is not bad at all…..

If it were, would we go DOWN on our knees and pray?

Would we celebrate a touch DOWN in a rugby match?

Why get relieved when the plane touches DOWN?

What is wrong with getting DOWN to basics?

Can we lift the car if the jack is not DOWN?

Now tell me, what is bad with DOWN
except the way you view it?

Is it not all in your head?

On a trampoline… staying static yields no fun. Force
yourself DOWN and the results will be fun. The harder
you force yourself DOWN the higher it will throw
you, higher than you could think you can go.

It is only when you are DOWN that you can look up.

When you are DOWN, there is only one
place for you to go, and that is UP!!!

DOWN is the place to be to gain strength to go UP.

When you are DOWN, turn up and see the stars. If
you can see the stars then you can reach them.

The only opportunity available to each one
of us when we are down is going up.

GO DOWN and work yourself UP.

FORGIVENESS

Who of us is perfect?

Who of us does not make mistakes?

You see, I have come to agree with those who say,

If you are afraid of making mistakes, the
sure way to do it is to do nothing.

Now with all of us busy with one thing or another,
and this includes but is not limited to:

- Lovingly engaged in household chores for your loved ones

- Running errands for the betterment of your family

- Engaging in a new career path

- Sharpening your skills to improve your income levels

- Doing your best to be the best partner for your spouse

- Going that extra mile for your folks
and the broader community.

In all the above and more, you are surely going to trample on some toes, over do or omit to do, execute certain things wrong and offend some people in the process, unintentionally most of the time. Sometimes you are going to be aware and sometimes not.

In times like these, the most beneficial and appropriate act would be to own up at the earliest or as soon as it is conveniently possible, as soon as you become aware.

This has nothing to do with your pride, so there is no need to swallow it. Keep your pride and politely say PLEASE FORGIVE ME.

If for any reason you find it difficult to ask for forgiveness, you are going to cause yourself, the other party and your relationship with the other party more harm than you can imagine.

Saying PLEASE FORGIVE ME enhances your image and show the people that you have offended that you do respect them.

You can only ask for forgiveness if you are prepared and willing to do so yourself.

As Mahatma Gandhi aptly states it when he says "The weak can never forgive. Forgiveness is the attribute of the strong."

We all should encourage one another to forgive, whether you are the perpetrator or the victim, because "Forgiveness is the fragrance that the violet sheds on the heel that crushed it" (Mark Twain) As perpetrator grabs the first opportunity to ask forgiveness and do not forget to forgive

yourself. It does not help much when the whole world
has forgiven you but you have not forgiven yourself

When we forgive or ask for forgiveness, we are by no
means looking at the past, we are actually paving the way
to the future. We must strive to be catalysts of forgiveness,
by allowing others an opportunity to exercise it on us
and for us to exercise it on those that offended us.

Forgiveness saves the heart from anger, hatred and wasted
spirit. It is the highest and final form of Love, and … need
I say it… IT IS FREE. Forgiveness is a virtue that is divine.
Is it not the first thing that Christ mentioned on the cross?

Forgiveness is by no means easy, and that is
precisely what makes it so important. It is not a
spontaneous action but a deliberate decision taken
with intent to free the soul and heal the wounds.

Forgive yourself by asking for forgiveness
and forgive those that have hurt you.

Sometimes, I dare say most of the times, we are hard on
ourselves, maybe even too hard.

We do not find it easy to forgive ourselves for the little torts
we commit. Whilst deep on our inside we know our imperfect
state, we nevertheless come hard on ourselves. We beg of others
to give us breaks which we deny ourselves.

Whilst we know that our lives are journeys to the city of perfect,
we hold our destinations too hard on our minds to the extent
of destabilising the journey.

Yes, I somewhat understand the saying that we should "fake
it till we make it", but I think we sometimes we fake it

dangerously too much. We fake it to the extent that in the process we become total fakes ourselves.

When we do not forgive ourselves, we remain in the state of imbalance. There is no internal harmony in us. We are internally not in sync. When in this state, can you imagine what signals we send to the world around us? (Our partners, children, colleagues, etc) What do we feed to our subconscious? and what do we attract into our lives.

This does not purport to be a lecture on the "Law of Attraction". I think we all know enough of that.

It comes to me as no surprise to see so many people unable to forgive.

If we do not learn to forgive ourselves, how can we be able to forgive others? Where do we get the training or the practice of doing this thing called forgiving if it does not begin in our innermost, doing it first to ourselves?

Yes, as the saying goes, "to err is human". We accumulate mistakes (of commission and omission) in the same manner that our bodies accumulate what causes us to need a bath each day. In like manner, we ought to take a self-forgiving bath at least (consciously so) once a day.

In this manner we will bless the world with a self-forgiven self who is capable, ready and willing to forgive the world.

This is what is divine in us.

It is divine because it liberates us to operate at full-throttle without guilt. It is divine because it attracts positiveness to us. It is divine because it liberates us from the state of perpetual guilt.

This state of guilt is evidenced by the suspicious looks we give to others and the negative perceptions we hold about them and the negative things we say about them. Further evidence is our obsession with how we look like on the outside (this includes obsession with material things) at the expense and price of our internal harmony. The picture of ourselves that we give to the outside world is pitted against the picture of our inner selves.

A forgiving heart forgives all the time.

Why all the time?

My assumption is based on the fact that we all say our daily morning prayer as our Good Lord taught his disciples (us). "Forgive us our trespasses, AS WE FORGIVE…….."

We daily commit ourselves to being agents of forgiveness.

If we fail, we fail ourselves.

What makes forgiving divine is the fact that we do it to those that hate us.

What wisdom is there in missing your blessings because of how you relate to those that hate you? Forgive them and free yourself to enjoy your blessings that you so richly deserve

We are blessed to the extent that we commit ourselves to things divine, with forgiveness being but one of them.

I have forgiven myself, have you?

SAY, THANK YOU

I have learnt and was told and came to understand that:

The one powerful word to use is: PLEASE

The two most rewarding words to use are: THANK YOU

The three most liberating words to use
are: PLEASE FORGIVE ME

If said with conviction, humility and from the
innermost, these words are able to free the soul.
A free soul is the beginning point of attaining
complete fulfilment. Isn't this what all of the human
race is yearning for? Fulfilment and freedom.

These three statements or utterances cannot be of any
effect whatsoever unless they be drawn from deep within
and said with the greatest sense of humility possible.

They evoke in those that receive or hear them, a great
measure of self-worth. They soften the heart. They have
the capacity to open doors that seem locked and sealed.

Do say THANK YOU to someone who has just
ordinarily greeted you and enquired about your health.
Whether he/she is a friend or a total stranger.

Do say THANK YOU to someone who takes your
call, whether in a friendly manner or otherwise.

Do say THANK YOU to a teller who serves you at a point
of sale irrespective of how you feel about the service.

Do say THANK YOU to anybody who interacts
with you in any manner whatsoever.

Do say THANK YOU for the dawn of a new
day, you have done nothing to deserve it.

Do say THANK YOU for the food
you eat, many go without.

Do say THANK YOU for the friends and family,
many are living theirs as lonely outcasts.

Do say THANK YOU for life and health… (Need I
say more …) you know your fortunes in this area.

Do say THANK YOU for the life and
health of family and friends.

Do say THANK YOU for the abundance
of opportunities around you.

Do say THANK YOU for Love and Peace.

In the words of Meister Eckhart "If the
only prayer you ever say in your entire life
is THANK YOU, it will be enough."

You cannot be too big or too small to say THANK YOU.

THANK YOU makes and keeps you big

Shower the great and the not-so-great with a big
THANK YOU to brighten your day and theirs.

THANK YOU opens doors.

THANK YOU strengthens.

THANK YOU attracts goodness into
otherwise gloomy lives.

THANK YOU enhances stature and self-worth.

THANK YOU said with humility, empowers.

Whether you say: *Ngiyabonga kakhulu,
inkomu, dankie, fofo, quyana,*

*mis takt, oshe, a dank aykh, nda kubiiri, kam sia,
enkosi kakhulu, diolch, merci, ndo livhuwa, spasibi,
jocolawal, nyeahweh, obrigada/o/u, salamat, dankie,
hvala, litumezi, ke a leboga, kashoonopihku, payla,
zikomo, natejchiri, mahalo, danksce ....etc,*
etc, etc. Whatever your native way it is of saying it,
say it from your heart. Just say it and see the world
unfold in a manner you never imagined possible.

As the saying goes "A rose by any name would smell as sweet", so spread the sweetness, say THANK YOU in any special way you can!!!

Make it a habit to tell people THANK YOU. To express your appreciation, sincerely and without the expectation of anything in return. Truly appreciate those around you, and you'll soon find many others around you. Truly appreciate life, and you'll find that you have more of it. Ralph Marston aptly states that we should "make it a habit".

Even "<u>The cock drinking water raises its head to God in THANKFULNESS</u>" (Ghana Proverb)

MISSING THE WOODS FOR THE TREES

Sitting in my sitting room, late in the afternoon, with the door open, absent minded and listening to the chirping of birds outside, I heard something like a small object hitting the window with a minute thud. It was not a loud sound but loud enough, in the silence I was sitting in, to take note of.

I quickly looked out and writhing in pain on the ground was a beautiful little bird.

I presumed it had crushed in full speed onto the windowpane of the closed window.

I said a little prayer wishing that it had not broken or fractured its tender neck or one of its vital little wings. It was a serious heartfelt prayer, maybe too big for the tiny little bird. The bird was the size of a recently hatched chick. It was wriggling on the one side, then turned over on the other side and ultimately on its back with its feet pointing upwards as though surrendering its soul to its creator.

A thought which I wished to suppress slipped my mind, and I whispered under my breath and to myself "it is dead".

Without moving, lest I added to its trauma, I strained my eyes to scrutinize the presence, or not, of any signs of life. To my relief I noticed some miniature heaving from its chest and abdomen, or should I say its torso?

I quietly stood up and tiptoed to fetch my mobile phone to use its camera part to capture this my privileged spectacle.

When I returned in less than a minute, it was on its legs, hunched and with pain written all over its tiny body. Not wanting to scare it off, I once more tiptoed to the window, which I so wished to blame but could not, that is cause of this misfortune. It was closed and the reflection of the sun falling on the bird made it impossible for me to catch a clear view of it.

As silently as I presumed a thief would do, I unlatched the opening part of the window. Windows normally give a click or squeak when being unlatched or opened. I vowed that this will not be the case this time. I feared that the little bird would fly away and I would lose the only moment of taking this rare picture.

As if my own life depended on it, I noiselessly unlatched the window. I was gripped by the anxiety that the hinges should not give a squeak lest I lose my moment. I loosened the sliding part and gently pushed the window open. Except the bright reflection that moved away from the bird, to my relief there was no sound at all. I took a few photos every time fearing that the almost absent click of the camera will scare it off.

With this being accomplished I tiptoed back to my seat to watch the total recovery of my friend, the unfortunate bird.

I am not very good at types and names of birds, so as I was holding my daytime vigil over my friend, I googled on my mobile for the identification of the bird. Now I could identify my friend, the bird, as the black–collared Barbet.

It started moving its head from side to side, scrutinizing its location. Seeing what looked like its misshapen beak whichI thought it had hurt or cracked at the moment of the impact. For a time I felt really sorry for it. I imagined how painful it is going to be for it to pick food up maybe it could even starve to death, I imagined.

I smiled alone with relief as it started making movements that indicated the somewhat ironic preparation for its imminent take off. The last thing I noticed before it finally took off was something falling off from its beak. My fears, so I thought, were realised that the poor bird is possibly going to starve to death, unable to pick up food for itself.

I stood up to pick up what I thought was to be the part of its broken beak. To both my surprise and relief, there was no piece of broken beak but a squirming twig-like little worm.

Like an accident reconstruction expert, I started reconstructing the circumstances that could have lead to my little bird crushing headlong onto the windowpane.

Being that late in the afternoon, I presumed it had not had a morsel since sunrise or for a long time, and it was desperately hungry. Perched on a branch it caught sight of a wormlike object on the ground and dove with lightning speed to catch its first meal for the day. With the catch in its beak and excitement in its heart, it became oblivious of its surroundings and lost its bearing as it took off to fly in haste. It is in this uncontrolled haste that it crushed into the windowpane which mirrored the vast open space which beckoned it to its illusionary bliss.

Lying in a dazed state on the ground with its tiny legs pointing skywards, it was wondering what has hit it. The poor little bird had at this moment forgotten about both its hunger and the yummy catch in its mouth. What mattered at that time was for it to regain its bearing and feel the wind under its wings. At this time, food was the least of its concerns. That is why the worm, that would have made a great meal for the day, fell off its beak as it took off to fly, happy to be alive. All else was of little or no importance at all.

Like a bolt of lightning, my old man's words of wisdom got a vivid illustration. When you unexpectedly get what you have sorely been yearning for, don't let such acquisition make you lose sight of the reality of your current situation and surroundings. Also do not forget who you are, where you come from, where you are in life and where you are heading to. Getting unexpected fortunes has the propensity to tempt people to react in an unusual and sometimes near suicidal manner. Such fortunes could be of any manner, mode or size.

Do we not at times behave in like manner? When hit by unexpected fortunes we forget about the realities of our circumstances and start, albeit for a moment, to walk with our heads in the clouds oblivious to the realities around us. We take unrealistic decisions that cause us to take actions with fatal or near fatal consequences to both ourselves and the loved ones around us. These are times when we can't see the woods for the trees.

Printed in the United States
By Bookmasters